THE DANGEROUS LIVES OF
HARP SEALS

BY MARY MEINKING

The
**Child's
World**®
childsworld.com

Published by The Child's World®
1980 Lookout Drive • Mankato, MN 56003-1705
800-599-READ • www.childsworld.com

Photographs ©: Jonathan Hayward/AP Images, cover, 1; Red Line Editorial, 5; Jupiter Images/PHOTOS.com>>/Thinkstock, 6, 9, 15; claumoho CC2.0, 8; Solent News/Rex Features/AP Images, 10; Florida Stock/iStockphoto, 11; Keith Monroe/Solent News/Rex Features/AP Images, 12; David White/ Rex USA, 16; Mike Price/Shutterstock Images, 19; iStockphoto, 20

Copyright © 2018 by The Child's World®
All rights reserved. No part of this book may be reproduced or utilized in any form or by any means without written permission from the publisher.

ISBN 9781503816251

33614080839839

LCCN 2016945621

Printed in the United States of America
PA02319

TABLE OF CONTENTS

FAST FACTS

Name

- Harp Seal (*Pagophilus groenlandicus*)

Diet

- Harp seals eat 120 species of fish, including cod, herring, halibut, and redfish.
- The seals also eat **crustaceans** such as krill and shrimp.

Average Life Span

- Harp seal pups face many dangers in the first weeks of their lives.
- If they reach adulthood, harp seals live for approximately 25 to 40 years.

Size

- Harp seals grow to be approximately 5.25 to 6.25 feet (1.6–1.9 m) long.

Weight

- Fully grown harp seals weigh approximately 250 to 300 pounds (110–140 kg).

Where They're Found

- Harp seals live near the edge of the Arctic sea ice so they can hunt in the ocean.

- In the summer, harp seals live in the Arctic. As the weather gets colder and the ice sheet grows, the seals **migrate** to the North Atlantic.

Harp seal habitats

Chapter 1

ABANDONED

A female harp seal swims through the cold waters of the North Atlantic Ocean. She looks around quickly. She is pregnant, and her seal pup is about to arrive. She needs to find an ice **floe** on which to give birth. The ice must be thick enough that it will not melt from under her.

Finally, she sees the perfect ice sheet. It is filled with hundreds of other harp seals. Some mothers are lying with their newborn pups. Others lie alone, awaiting their pups' arrivals. All the seals are marked with a black "harp," or a saddle-like shape on their backs.

The late-arriving female swims over to the ice floe. She claws her way out of the water. She then wiggles across the ice to the **whelping** grounds.

◄ Harp seals spend most of their time in the water. But they need solid ice on which to give birth and raise pups.

The female returns to the area each year. There is less ice available each time she returns. Global warming has also caused the ice to melt earlier. The female settles in an area with thicker ice that is also protected from the gusting winds.

▲ **Harp seals often return to the same whelping grounds each year.**

▲ A pup's white coat helps keep it warm until the seal can develop fat.

Within a few hours, she delivers a fluffy white pup. The skinny "whitecoat" pup begins to shiver in the frigid air. The mother snuggles with her pup to warm him. Soon the pup begins to nurse. He feeds six to seven times each day. His mother's milk is 45 percent fat. The pup gains 5 pounds (2.3 kg) per day. All he does is eat and sleep.

▲ **Pups are left unprotected when their mothers hunt.**

After a few days, the mother wiggles across the ice and slides into the water. She is hungry and needs to find something to eat. But when she returns, all the pups look alike. Which one is hers? She listens for her pup's cry. She sniffs the air for her pup's scent. Soon the two are reunited for another feeding.

By day 12, the pup has tripled his birth weight. He now has a thick layer of **blubber**. The blubber will help keep him warm in the frigid winds and water.

It is time for the mother to **wean** her pup. She gives him one last nuzzle. Then she turns and wiggles into the water. The pup will never see her again. Can the tiny pup survive in this frozen environment on his own?

▲ Once pups develop a layer of blubber, their mothers leave them on their own.

Chapter 2

THE HUNTED

The pup is hungry. With nothing to eat and no one to protect him, he lies on the ice and cries loudly. Within days, he starts to **molt**. Patches of the pup's fluffy white coat fall off. Underneath is short, gray fur. The short fur will make it easier for the pup to swim.

After two weeks without eating, the pup wiggles closer to the water. He looks over the edge of the ice for fish. Soon he spies some tiny krill swimming by. He leans over the edge to reach them. As he does, his front flippers fall off the edge. The pup splashes into the water. He begins slapping his front flippers on the surface to stay afloat. It works. He's swimming!

◀ Harp seals that are learning to swim are called "beaters" because they beat at the water to stay afloat.

The splashing seal pup starts to gain some control in the water. He swims in circles and begins to slurp up some nearby krill. But he tires quickly. He claws his way back onto the ice to rest. After a couple of weeks' practice, the pup is a good hunter.

One day, the pup is awoken by a loud scraping sound. A large ship has pulled next to his ice floe. He sees men with clubs dashing onto the ice. They chase after the pups. The men are sealers. They hunt pups to use their **pelts** and blubber.

The men approach the pup. He has never seen humans before. The pup senses danger. The other pups yowl, and the men holler to one another. The pup wiggles closer and closer to the edge of the ice. At the last moment, the pup slides into the water, away from the sealers. The pup will need to find a new home.

Pups' white jackets are replaced with short, gray fur. ▶
This is when sealers hunt them.

Chapter 3

UNDERWATER DANGERS

The seal pup bobs in the water along with several others. The young pups join together to form a small herd. Instinct kicks in, and the young harp seals begin their first long migration north. They are heading to the summer feeding grounds in the Arctic. Food is plentiful there.

The seal pup hunts during the day. His bullet-shaped body shoots underwater after fish and crustaceans. The pup surfaces every 10 minutes to breathe. Once his stomach is full, he sleeps while floating in the water. When darkness arrives, he joins the other pups and swims north through open water.

◄ **Harp seals hunt during the day, when it is light enough to see fish and shrimp. The seals migrate at night.**

One day, the pup and the other young seals come across a school of Atlantic cod. The cod are bunched together. They are easy targets. The seal dives and eats as many fish as he can.

Suddenly a woven wall comes toward the pup. It is a fishing net. Similar to the harp seals, fishermen are trying to catch the school of Atlantic cod. The pup turns and shoots away from the net. He escapes and swims far away into the open ocean. A few other seals in the group do not make it. They get caught in the net and drown.

After months of travel, the young seal reaches the Arctic feeding grounds. It is summertime. The water and sea ice are filled with thousands of harp seals of all ages. The young pup has traveled more than 1,500 miles (2,400 km). He is exhausted and needs to eat as much as he can. He needs to build up blubber that will keep him warm in winter.

One warm evening, the growing young pup bobs in the water with his fellow harp seals.

▲ The orca whale is one of the harp seal's natural predators.

A large dark shape catches his eye. It is moving closer and closer to the group. It is an orca whale! At the last moment, the **predator** opens its giant mouth.

The pup shoots away. The orca snaps its jaw shut but misses the young seal. The other pups rocket away, too. The pup zigzags through the water with the orca right behind him. After a short chase, he loses the orca.

▲ As the winter ice grows, harp seals must migrate south to have access to open water.

Predators such as orca whales, Greenland sharks, and walruses **prey** on harp seals in the Arctic waters. On the ice, polar bears prowl for young seals.

Within a couple of months, the weather turns cold. The young seal and the others begin their long migration southward ahead of the new-forming ice.

There will be more food to the south in the winter. The young seal survived many dangerous encounters during his first year. He learned from each challenge. These helped prepare him for life in the Arctic.

THINK ABOUT IT

- Global warming is reducing the world's ice floes. But harp seals depend on ice. Can you name the times that the harp seals need ice?
- The Canadian government, among others, limits the number of harp seals that can be killed each year. It also controls the age of the seals hunted and the method used to kill them. Should governments continue to control the hunting of harp seals? Why or why not?
- Harp seals face both natural and human-made challenges. What are some examples of both?

GLOSSARY

blubber (BLUB-ur): Blubber is fat under the skin of a marine animal. The harp seal has a layer of blubber to keep it warm in the freezing water.

crustaceans (kruh-STAY-shuhns): Crustaceans are sea creatures with outer skeletons. The harp seal often eats crustaceans.

floe (FLOH): A floe is a large sheet of ice. A harp seal needs an ice floe on which to give birth and raise its young.

migrate (MYE-grate): To migrate is to move from one place to another. Harp seals start to migrate in the fall.

molt (MOHLT): To molt is to lose a covering of fur, feathers, or hair and replace it with new growth. Harp seals molt every year to get a new coat of fur.

pelts (PELTS): Pelts are outer skins with hair, wool, or fur. Sealers sell harp seal pelts for money.

predator (PRED-uh-tur): A predator is an animal that kills and eats other animals. A shark is a predator of harp seals.

prey (PRAY): To prey on something is to hunt and kill it for food. Orca whales prey on harp seals.

wean (WEEN): To wean is to stop feeding an animal its mother's milk. Harp seals wean their pups quickly.

whelping (WELP-ing): Whelping is the process of giving birth. Female harp seals give birth in areas called whelping grounds.

TO LEARN MORE

Books

Drumlin, Sam. *Harp Seals.* New York: PowerKids, 2013.

King, Aven. *Harp Seals.* New York: PowerKids, 2016.

Simon, Seymour. *Global Warming.* New York: Harper Collins, 2010.

Web Sites

Visit our Web site for links about harp seals:

childsworld.com/links

Note to Parents, Teachers, and Librarians: We routinely verify our Web links to make sure they are safe and active sites. So encourage your readers to check them out!

SELECTED BIBLIOGRAPHY

Hammill, M. O., and G. B. Stenson. "Changes in Ice Conditions and Potential Impact on Harp Seal Pupping." *Fisheries and Ocean Canada.* Government of Canada, Aug. 2014. Web. 22 Jul. 2016.

"Harp Seal." *Seal Conservation Society.* Seal Conservation Society, Sep. 2011. Web. 22 Jul. 2016.

"Harp Seals." *NOAA Fisheries.* National Oceanic and Atmospheric Administration, 15 Jan. 2015. Web. 22 Jul. 2016.

INDEX

ABOUT THE AUTHOR

Mary Meinking is a graphic designer who writes children's books in her spare time. She has written more than 30 nonfiction books on many different topics. Mary keeps busy working, writing, and hanging out with her family in Iowa. She also enjoys making crafts, taking photos, baking, and traveling.